Planting seeds of hope, curiosity, courage, and connection
For all of life
For Samuel and Noah

Acclaim for **The Apple in the Orchard**

"The Apple in the Orchard by Sonia Di Maulo is a lovely little book with a profound message: To pursue greatness, aspiring leaders sometimes must dare to leave the familiar. Opportunities for growth and learning are all around you—so take the leap, and grow!"

Ken Blanchard | Coauthor of *The One Minute Manager®* **and** *Great Leaders Grow*

"Sonia has crafted a unique 'food-for-thought' story that gets at the heart of what it takes to work together as teams, workplaces, as well as families. Read it; chew on it; and harvest it!"

Roy Saunderson | President, Recognition Management Institute

"Organizations need to empower each individual employee to lead in order to impact the overall organization. The Apple in the Orchard illustrates that with courage and the right environment each individual can lead and influence others."

François Barbeau | Regional Operations Manager, Future Shop

"Metaphor is a powerful way to help us think and learn. In this short book, Sonia presents a metaphor for leadership, organizations, human behavior and more. And in the best use of metaphor, the lessons are yours to find. Read and think; seek and find!"

Kevin Eikenberry | Bestselling Author of *Remarkable Leadership* **and** *From Bud to Boss*

"The Apple in the Orchard reminds me of Mark Twain's quote: "Courage is resistance to fear, mastery of fear, not absence of fear." Read it and it will inspire your courage."

John M. Bernard | Author of *Business at the Speed of Now*

"A fable for all ages. Truth resides and resonates."

S. Max Brown | Principal, Leadership Initiatives at Rideau Recognition

"More than anyone I know, Sonia understands and illustrates the power and benefit of collaboration, feedback and teamwork. Even through the illustration of an apple orchard, you will find lessons and reminders about the importance of working unselfishly toward a goal for the success of the team. Simple, yet profound!"

Mike Henry Sr. | Founder, Lead Change Group

"The Apple in the Orchard" is a clever allegory about how leaders can inspire individuals to ripen for peak performance. At their core the best apples contain seeds to nurture knowledge-sharing and a resilient skin. Employees are not left to shrivel on Pale Green waiting to be harvested."

Karen Carleton | MEd., MS Performance Solutions Corp.

"This book's evocative agrarian imagery advances a message that's vital to any leadership endeavor: feel the fear and do it anyway."
Jennifer V. Miller | Founder, The People Equation blog

"A lovely fable about coming alive and growing into an interconnected, flourishing world. This personal journey is one that each of us must take to realize an environmentally sustainable, socially just and spiritually fulfilling human presence on this planet."
Kathryn A. Cooper | B.Sc., MBA, M.Ed. President & Chief Learning Officer, Sustainability Learning Centre

"In this profound and poignant fable, Sonia Di Maulo beautifully illustrates the power of courage in pursuing our dreams. Sometimes all we need is just one moment of insane courage in which we let go of the familiar, and as Brave Apple learns, that one moment makes all the difference."
Jane Perdue | Principle, Braithwaite Innovation Group

"I love "The Apple in the Orchard" with its layers of inspiration, hope, and the lesson that "harvest" comes from connection. And I adore "Brave Apple" as she reminds us all that "Hearts filled with courage can rise to any challenge."
Thomas Waterhouse | Principal, Simple E Creations, Inc.

"Brave Apple gives readers something to aspire to and hope for. She casts a vision for emerging leaders and provides an example that we can all benefit from emulating. Sonia's poetic leadership metaphor is beautifully carried out in The Apple in the Orchard. Her writing is purposeful, impactful and further brought to life by the vibrant graphics of this book."
Erin Schreyer | CLTMC President, Sagestone Partners, LLC

"The Apple In the Orchard reminds me of a favorite quote from Albert Einstein, "If you can't explain it to a 6 year old, you don't understand it yourself." The story and the illustrations are simple enough to be a child's bedtime story, challenging enough to be shared in an executive boardroom and inspiring enough to be read and savored again, and again, and again. A perfect gift for yourself and for those you love and serve."
Chery Gegelman | President, Giana Consulting

"I love The Apple in the Orchard! The illustrations and story ignite a powerful message for leaders. Share this story with every aspiring and emerging leader you know!"
Becky Robinson | Principle, Weaving Influence

Thanks to
Constantina Kalimeris, Michelle Holliday, Ida, Teresa,
Don Di Maulo, and Sandro Cappadoro.

Special thank you to my mom, Olga Di Maulo,
who inspired me with the gift of courage.

The Apple in the Orchard

A story about finding the courage to emerge as a leader

By Sonia Di Maulo

Illustrations by Constantina Kalimeris

The Apple in the Orchard
www.theappleintheorchard.ca

Text © 2012 Sonia Di Maulo
ISBN 978-0-988-05460-8
Illustrations © 2012 Constantina Kalimeris

Published in Canada by:
Harvest Performance
www.harvestperformance.ca

Harvest
Performance

First electronic edition published in Montreal, Quebec, April 2012.
First printed edition published in Montreal, Quebec, September 2012.

The artwork in this book was rendered using color pencils and digital media.
The text is set in Gill Sans.
Designed by Constantina Kalimeris.

Foreword

For such a simple story, The Apple in the Orchard is rich with meaning, carrying important implications for every level of our lives – from the personal to the organizational to the planetary.

At the broadest level, Sonia Di Maulo's engaging little tale focuses our attention on the integral, interdependent nature of all life, including our own.

This insight may be unfamiliar to some. Most of us were raised to believe that all forms of life are inherently separate from each other and that they interact with their environment in a basic, surface-level exchange of resources. The machine has been our dominant guiding metaphor, with everything in the universe thought to operate like clockwork. According to that story, understanding the parts of anything meant that we understood everything there was to know about the whole.

As you will see, this is the story of poor Pale Green, who sees herself as separate from the other trees in the orchard and who lives without purpose beyond survival.

Over the past several decades, however, science has revealed that there is much more to the story – that the entire biosphere forms such a profoundly interdependent web that we can be considered distinct but not truly separate from our living surroundings. It has shown that, in living systems, the whole is much more than the sum of the parts. And though there are mechanistic characteristics in every living system, we've begun to see that these are not their most interesting or important features.

These are the lessons that Brave Apple comes to understand as she discovers that she is an inextricable part of a living whole. In opening up to this aspect of her existence, she is able to gain access to the collective intelligence of the entire orchard ecosystem. More than that, she is able to tap into the life that flows throughout the orchard. And she glows.

For each of us, the implications are significant. First, Brave Apple's adventure points to the importance of living with purpose. Many of us share her yearning to connect, to belong, to contribute to the whole of life, and in these ways to feel life's vitality flow freely through us. But it takes courage to move away from the old machine story of competition and consumption and instead to move toward life-enhancing connectedness and contribution. Often, as with Brave Apple, it takes a leap of faith.

Her experience also invites us to consider how we, too, can access the intelligence of our living surroundings. What reflective practices will allow us to tune in to our instincts and inspirations, so that we can deeply know what is needed and what is ours to contribute?

Perhaps even more significant — and important -- are the implications for our organizations. The Apple in the Orchard hints at different ways of working together, united by purpose, trusting in each other, communicating freely and collaborating creatively. It inspires us with Red Harvest's example of wise stewardship. It sets a high bar for our organizations: just as the trees in the story seek to contribute to the well being of the entire orchard, every organization is invited to contribute to the well being and resilience of its community and, indeed, of the whole of life. And in aiming for this higher goal, Brave Apple's experience assures us that we, and our organizations can thrive more fully in the process. There is no compromise.

These lessons come at a critical time. There is a clear link between our failure to recognize the fundamental integrality of life and our diminishing ability to support life sustainably. And there is just as clear a connection between viewing ourselves as isolated, competing metabolism machines and our growing discontent –"the disenchantment of the world," as sociologist Max Weber called it.

For humanity, and even for most organizations, the challenges we face are too complex and too urgent to solve with individual intellect alone. What is needed is the wisdom and speed of self-organizing collective intelligence in support of individual initiative. Working, thinking and reacting collectively is a hallmark of living systems -- consider the speed with which the individual cells of your body self-organize to react collaboratively to an injury or an invading virus. The survival of our organizations -- and, more importantly, of humanity -- demands that we learn to understand and work deliberately with this powerful capability that comes with being alive.

The task for us in the emerging era is to participate consciously in the full pattern of life. In expanding our view beyond the role of the individual, we can recognize the vast opportunities to connect and collaborate. We can open our perception to the will and wisdom of the whole. And most of all, we can craft the necessary conditions to engage the human spirit, with all its creative power.

What could be more important than that?
The heart of the matter is the need for conversation about what makes us alive, creative and connected, particularly in our organizations. That is the core invitation of this book.

Michelle Holliday

Michelle Holliday is an organizational strategy consultant based in Montreal. For the past fifteen years, she has conducted extensive research into the patterns of living systems, including organizations, economies and civilizations. She is a frequent writer and presenter, as well as author of the forthcoming book, Humanity 4.0. She can be reached at michelle@cambiumconsulting.com.

It's almost time for the annual harvest.

People from all over will come to enjoy the quiet beauty of the orchard;

to select and savor the juicy goodness of the fruit. Before the harvest begins, the

farmer selects apples from several trees in the orchard. He wants to ensure the

apples are growing as he intended.

It is an honor to be part of an orchard that is connected in purpose.

This orchard's purpose is clear—to produce an abundance of healthy fruit that

sustains life. This is the orchard's unique and meaningful contribution.

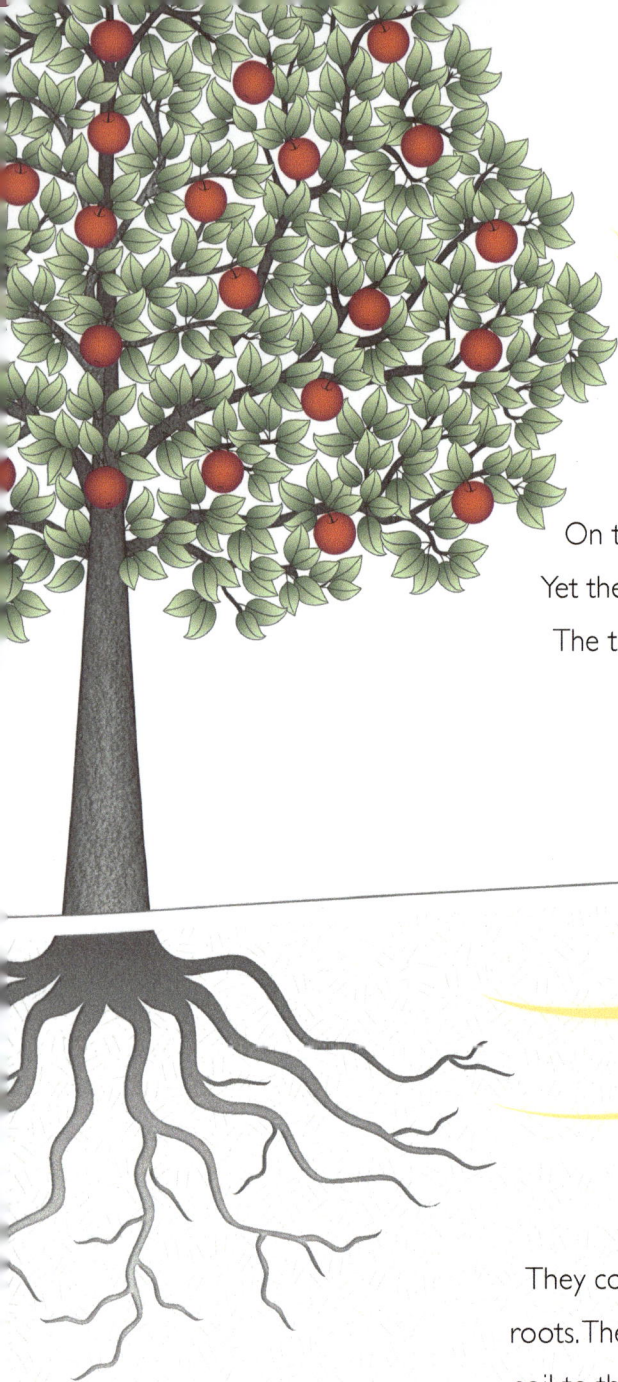

On the surface, the trees appear to be separate and independent.
Yet they actively collaborate with each other and all life on the planet.
The trees' connection is silent, and the messages that travel through
and between them are undetected by their visitors.

They are connected underground:
They communicate their growth through a web of fungi that unites their
roots. The fungi absorb and transport water, oxygen, and minerals from the
soil to the roots, to the trunk, to the branches, to the leaves, to the apples.

They are connected above:

Messages transmitted via chemicals sway through the air from one tree

to the other through their leaves.

The connection begins with the strongest tree in the orchard;

the tree that connects all the others.

Her name is Red Harvest.

She nurtures the connections and cultivates collaboration. This is the tree from which all future apple trees are grown. As the mother tree, she cares for the health of the whole orchard hoping to reach all trees through the fungal network.

Red Harvest's messages spread easily and quickly, cultivating a glow in the orchard.

As with all messages, though, they are sometimes received yet not believed. This is true in the outermost parts of the orchard. There, the idea of trees collaborating to sustain life through their apples seems unnatural. Each tree works independently. The drive to contribute is lost.

Pale Green is a young tree at the top of the hill. He grows at the far end of the orchard.

Pale Green's apples are small, dull, and soft to the touch. Their seeds are shriveled and nearly devoid of life.

The tree lost his belief in the interconnection of all life on earth. Without this, Pale Green thinks he is separate and completely independent. The messages and support from the orchard are lost too. His apples struggle. They still hope to be picked; they grow in the best way they know how.

Brave Apple grows on Pale Green.

From her branch, she can see the whole orchard.

Brave Apple can see Red Harvest's glow, but she cannot feel it.

Like many of the apples in the orchard, Brave Apple is irresistibly drawn to her.

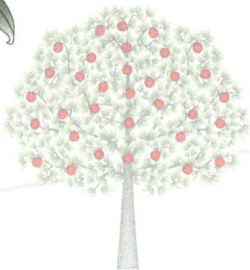

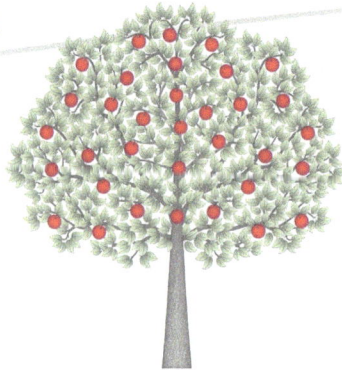

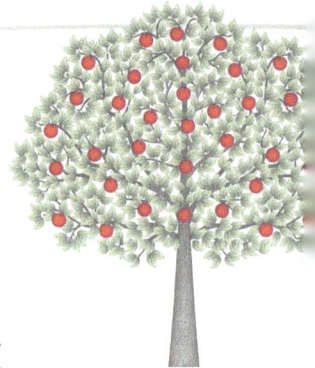

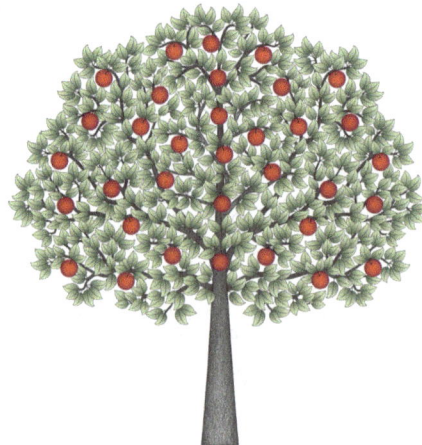

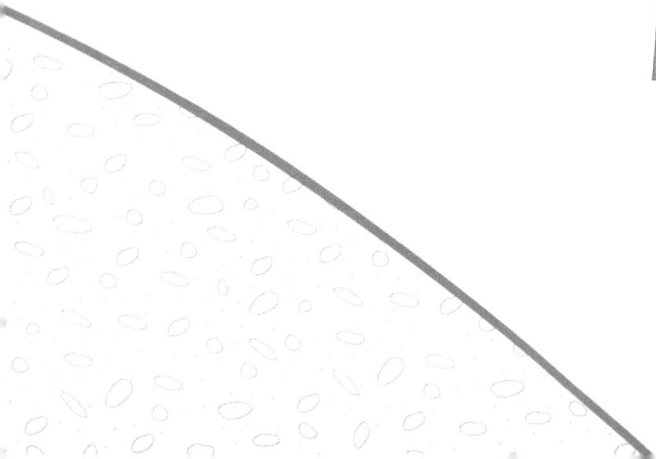

A desire to connect to Red Harvest overwhelms Brave Apple.
To learn more about the life that surrounds the beautiful tree, Brave
Apple will have to get closer.
"Should I risk it?" she asks herself.
"Should I take the leap to learn more?"

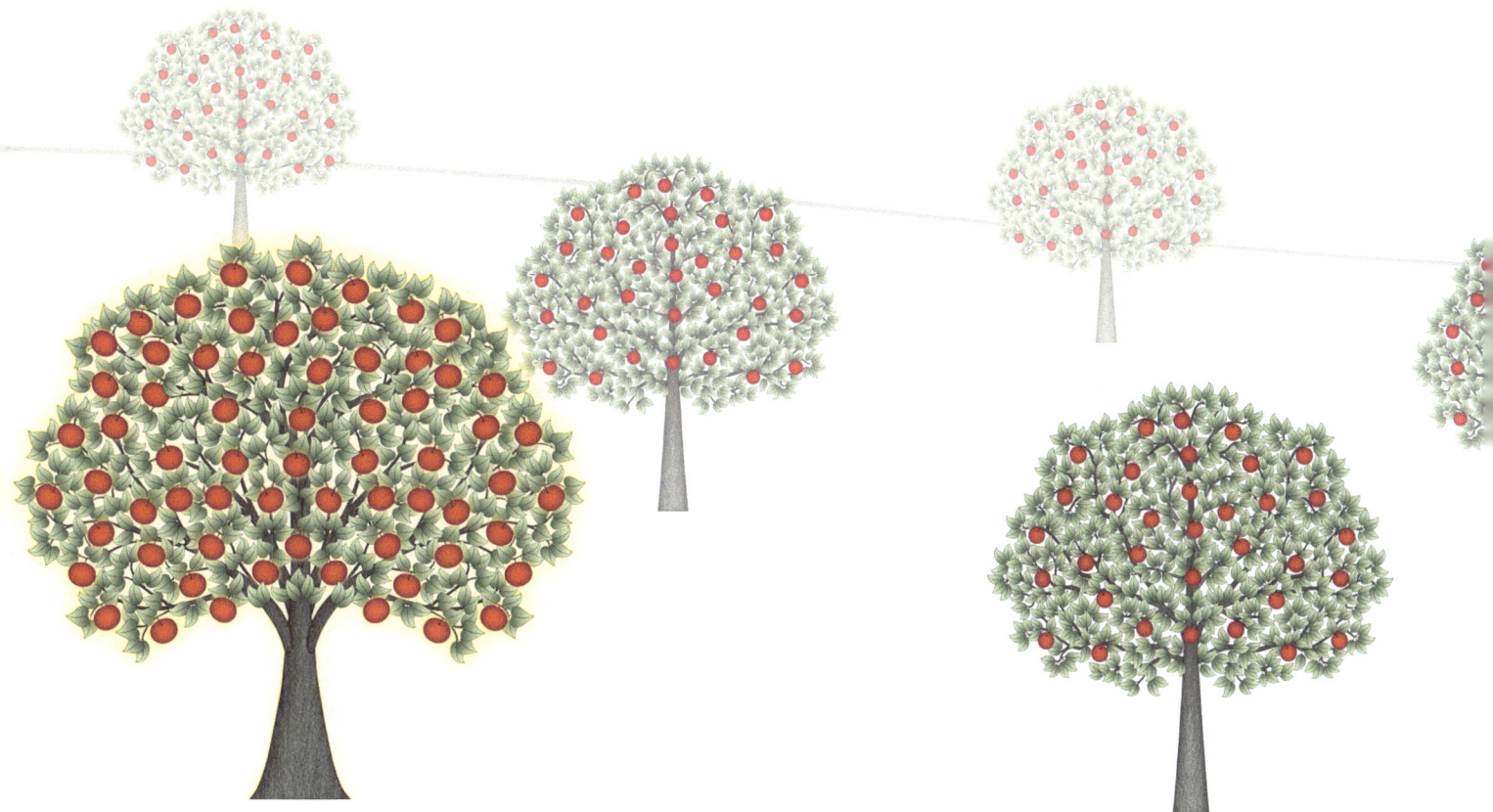

Brave Apple listens to the truth within her.

Her decision is clear.

She twists and turns until she pops free from her branch.

In that falling moment, she hears all of Pale Green – the leaves, branches, and other apples – gasp.

The surrounding trees sway in her direction as if to propel her toward her quest.

In that moment, the story of the Brave Apple becomes legend.

Down the hill she rolls and rolls, until she
meets Red Harvest's radiance.

She snuggles against the tree's trunk and feels
the energy she once could only see.

She sighs happily, exhausted, but unable to rest.
Her desire to learn is overwhelming.

Brave Apple doesn't know what she is searching
for, yet in her core she knows she did the right thing,
that she is where she needs to be.

She watches, listens, and feels, trying to learn
the secret of the glowing tree.

Being so close to the earth that surrounds Red Harvest, Brave Apple feels the messages communicated to and from the roots. She feels the energy that connects the trees. And she sees what she hadn't seen before. All around Red Harvest, the other trees are glowing too.

Red Harvest is sharing her secret and she listens and accepts feedback in return.

The messages underground and above are arriving, urgent and clear. The earth lifts the little apple as Red Harvest's roots reach out. A windstorm is coming. The nearby trees heed her warning, and the apples, leaves, and roots around her hold on.

Brave Apple's life on Pale Green seems so far away now. Even as her own life begins to fade, she feels the strength, connection and life of the trees around her.

The day is hot and Red Harvest's leaves are losing water. The signal is perfect; from her branches it reaches her roots with the message to take in more water. Then the earth becomes thirsty; Red Harvest's roots release a signal to her leaves asking them to close their pores so they won't lose even more precious water. Balance is restored.

The harmony between the earth and the apples washes over Brave Apple.
Though her end is near, she becomes brighter.
She begins to glow.

Brave Apple feels alive next to Red Harvest.

The apple reaches deep within her core and does something the trees will tell stories about.

She sends her own signal throughout the orchard. The signal is strong; the answer is provided.

She believes.

Brave Apple is ready. For whatever lies ahead of her, she is at last ready.

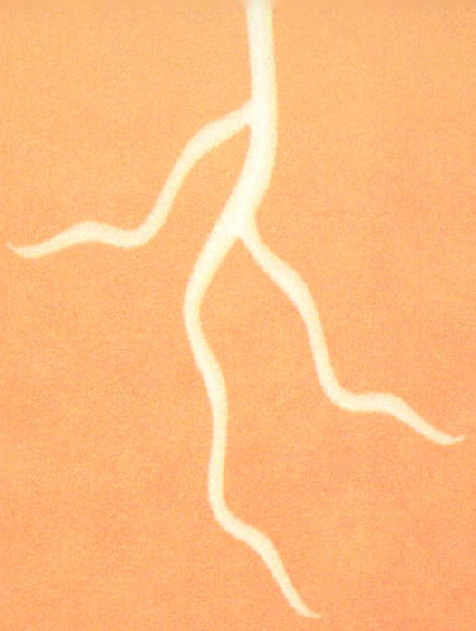

What are **you** ready for?

Get Ready to Emerge!

The road to successful leadership begins with awareness of self, environment, people, and the relationships connecting us all. We have lost our natural ability to connect and collaborate in a way that acknowledges and sustains the interconnection of all life on earth.

Sonia Di Maulo guides individuals, teams, and organizations through a rediscovery of our natural ability to work in a meaningful way; to listen and accept the desire and courage to emerge (both ours and that of others). This emergence is essential to innovate, collaborate, grow, and sustain healthy workplaces of the future.

Successful organizations listen to emerging leaders (of all ages) and build processes of collaboration. Brave Apple is not alone. As her story becomes legend, many follow her lead and help the orchard to thrive through innovation and new ways of working together. This is how the orchard keeps evolving to maintain its resilience. This orchard can be your organization.

Through keynotes, workshops, and leadership coaching, learn how to model living systems and develop a plan towards the new, sustainable world of work. Join The Harvest Performance mailing list and get access to a free workbook: **www.harvestperformance.ca**

Cultivate the courage to emerge in your people. To purchase The Apple in the Orchard for the Brave Apples in your organization, visit **www.theappleintheorchard.ca**